Flotsam and Jetsam

JODY EMOND

Hay River Books • Montreal

ISBN 978-0-9736561-3-8 (paperback)

Set in 11/13 Book Antiqua by Hay River Books
Cover illustration by Dave Yuden

For Sabrina

To show a little of what I was,
what I am, and what I am becoming

ALONE in my solitude
is where i stand
without pain
or pleasure
without joy
or sadness
with nothing
existing in neutrality

TEARING through the madness, i find
tranquility
peace
quiet
a subjective reality in which
the world is mine

distorted faces
shadows without bodies
dancing in the darkness
aimless desolation
void of meaning
keep out the light

no direction
freedom to die

1

HERE i sit
in the solitude of my insanity
my mind loses its grip
on reality
my heart its purity
or maybe
i am finally seeing
and feeling clearly
such are the paradoxes

MY mind expands like a web
in infinite directions
like a spider
i devour all that touches it
becoming one with all
that i ingest

i become myriad selves
losing myself in the minds and souls
of others

where am i?
who am i?
where am i going?
questions of the ages

Jody Emond

I SEEK myself
only to find a void

perhaps i do not exist

MY spirit screams
to be heard
yearns to be touched

how long has it been?
how long will it be?

i feel all that touches me
my heart fills with love
and with sadness
my eyes fill with tears

i feel the beauty, i see the joy
experiencing the world to its fullest
through that which makes me human
my heart

LIKE a shadow of what i could be
i see his face
knowing that reality
will never let me

the multitudes of me fight for control
but the force that gives them their strength
also has a mind of its own

THE emptiness is alive and well
spreading through my heart

it carries the cold, hard vacuum of this world
try to hide the pain, shut it in
smother it
drown it in hedonism

it doesn't matter how hard you try
it always finds a way
it peeks out and lets you know
it's there
waiting, knowing
that your moment of weakness will come

it will have life again
your life

Jody Emond

I AM wrong
or so they believe

i know i am right
my aims are true
my beliefs are just

my goal is the betterment
of all concerned

when will they see
when will they hear
that my words are true
and right?

we live in the greyness of uncertainty
in the solitude of anonymity
each seeking our way
in the darkness of despair
alone
in a world of me

why is it
we can't reach out as brothers
in spirit and loving understanding?

REALITY is like rubber to be bent at your will
if only you have the strength
to do it

fuck 'em all
save yourself
they can't and don't want to be saved

I THANK you parents
for the insanity
you have bequeathed me
although it is not a joyous gift
it is at least an interesting one

THE words can't last forever
i wish they could
but their time is short-lived
existing in a multitude of frames
to come and go

the feelings rise and subside
like the waves of the infinite ocean
always to return

sometimes i wish i could keep them
these feelings
the oscillations of life
infinite in time and space

HYPOCRITES
liars
betrayers
stab you in the back
whenever it's expedient

say one thing
and mean another
the scalpel that promises to save you
can also kill

you trusted them
you loved them
but what a mistake

now you are alone with nowhere to go
no one with which to share yourself

who are these deserters you believed in?
why, they are your friends and lovers
hypocrites
liars
betrayers

THE time has come
for the flower to expand its pedals
for the ocean to make its waves

like all things born
it too must grow
live to its potential

arise and stand
son of man
your time has come
feel your destiny pulling
make the changes
answer the call, wait no longer
time grows short
and the need grows greater

strength
fragility
complex yet
simple
potential in its rawest form

what will become of him?
only those who mould him know
a god, a devil
a peasant, a king?

only the ticks and tocks
of the clock will tell

Jody Emond

SITTING here
alone
watching the electric dragon go by
i wonder
where we are
and where we are going
will we arrive at our destination whole
or more than we are now?

unlike life
the steel road of the dragon
is fixed, unswerving
impossible to deviate from

if only life were so

HERE i sit on the precipice
of my insanity
my masochistic tendencies
enticing me
to commit the ultimate act

SURROUNDED by the infidels
of intellect and soul
i must find my way to my higher destiny

stick me in the heart
laugh at my name
the shame won't be mine for long
soon it shall be yours
when i am where i am going
and you are still where you were

WORDS
creeping through my mind
aimlessly and thoughtlessly
bombarding my senses
trying to bring order to the raw impulses
trying to save me from the confusion of myself

THE blinding light of insanity
envelops my mind
like a blanket of confusion
myriad forms, cascading colours
assaulting my senses
confusion

disorientation
become one with me
where am i
amidst these never-ending waves of terror?

EVEN though
i sit here in my solitude
i relish the fact
that those around me
are joining in the soul
and in the spirit

such is the beauty
such is that which makes us human

THE insanity of others is easy to understand
once you have understood your own

standing alone
seeking the answers in every direction
i grow only more confused
and alone

i have sought inward
only to find a question
i have sought outward
only to find solitude
where must i seek the answers
that will save me?

I AM the sheep
who seeks to be the ram
aside the cliff
horns of pearly white innocence
bravely ignoring
the dangers
of my precarious situation

TIME stands still
in this twisted reality
everything is so
slow

Jody Emond

SIFTING through the sands
of my once-fertile mind
i come across some ancient belief
once it was strong
based on what seemed
the firmest of grounds
now
the ravages of time
have worn it down
to dust
like ancient man
forsaken
in the name of evolution

spinning and twisting
is my soul
in this reality created for me
oppression
compression
limiting me
i seek to expand
to spread my limbs

MY dreams may be far
they may be out of my grasp
but as long as they carry me
to my full potential
i shall continue
to have and to hold them
for they are my strength and direction

IN this lost wilderness of humanity
i seek to find my true self
slowly i find the pieces of the puzzle
that is me

with satisfaction
i assemble them
feeling
that the pieces shall form a picture
of subtle beauty
the whole world
shall gaze upon

Jody Emond

THOUGH now i stand alone
in this solitude
you created for me
i realize that what wasn't
was never meant to be

staring into the blackness
i see a distorted picture of myself
filled with hatred, anger, pain
how to reconcile these feelings
so i may go on
into the light
that though i cannot see
i know is there

-

THE burden of my past weighs me down
the immoveable mass of the future facing me

so despite my struggle to move on
i stand still
going nowhere

FUMBLING my way
through the twisted reality
of the night
i find a path
filled with distorted shadows
my mind altered
my true self unveiled
i savour this freedom
the freedom of inebriation

I LOOKED into the mirror
to see myself as i really was
twisted, distorted, unlovable
then this man came along
"hey buddy, move," he said

as i did, he removed the mirror
putting another in its place

looking anew
i saw that i was not
what i thought i was
i was beautiful
a symbol
of greatness and goodness
a god among men
and i realized a new hope

like a dream i float
in this new reality
ever seeking the strength
that will carry me
through the gates
to the future
to the promised land
to the place where my hopes
 and desires reside
where i can be at peace
with myself
may i never wake up

I AWOKE this morning
with no memory of who i was
only with the knowledge
of what
and who i am
and
can be

I LOST yesterday
only to find tomorrow

YELLOW
all pervasive
all encompassing
filling me with hope
warmth, energy, strength
power
to accomplish all

possibilities
limitless
renewal
reconstruct
novelty
explore
feel
experience
challenge
go and seek
illumination
without end

you will not bring me down
i am my own adversity
i am my own best friend
my own worst enemy
i am my one true inspiration

Jody Emond

IN this torment
i seek my way out
only to find
that none exists
forever i must wallow
in this mire of filth
with these wretched ones
their eyes so accustomed
to the blandness
of their own hearts and souls
that they cannot see the light
they are dead
yet still walking
thinking they are alive

THIS insanity
is one to be shared
one to be enjoyed

embrace its escape
the freedom to see clearly
walk through the rose-coloured clouds
of the mind
swim in the infinite ocean
of the soul

all the doors are open
step through one

STEPPING outside this house
i raise my face
to the warm yellow sun
feeling its radiance
bathing me in love
energizing my soul
i embrace my god
cherishing this sense of oneness

standing alone in the
twisted, swirling darkness
of our confusion
we search the sky
of our mind's eye
for the stars
that will light the way
to hope

like the ancient sailors
of times gone by
we are lost on this ocean
without the stars' light
to show us the way
to our destination

so we sail
the infinite seas
of life and universe
without direction or goal

Jody Emond

-

LIKE a muse
of days gone by
she inspires
and enlightens me
a spring of hope
a world of faith
she gives me
renewed beliefs
renewed chances

STANDING there
in the eye of the storm
i found her
welcome relief
in a world gone mad
the sole comfort
the only truth

i rejoice
in her presence
like a gift from beyond

i dive into the possibilities
may the gods be merciful

SEEING the rift
i built a bridge
only to realize
i was too afraid
to cross

THE soaring spirit
knows no bounds
the skies are infinite
as are the possibilities
that exist between
you
and i

THE lights
blind me
the music
is only noise
the people
are strangers
the calm
the warmth
of honesty
are welcomed
with relief

I LOOKED into the twin mirrors
that are her eyes
and saw an image of myself
i heard the echo
of my mind
in her voice
souls that touch
minds that are one
and finally i realized
that though i stand in solitude
i shall never be alone
for in my mind
lies the memory of her beauty

the feelings fade
of my pleasure and pain
no longer shall i yearn
for the unreachable
nor shall i live in the reaching

gone is the discomforting incertitude of being
replaced by the comfort of oblivion
gone is the questioning of the future
supplanted by the answers
of the present

reluctantly
i return to the flock
awaiting the day
when i shall be the shepherd

WE stand
suspended in mid-air
above the black abyss
desperately searching for something
with which to support ourselves
fearing
that if we do not
we shall fall into this
the endless well of self

"I" RESOUNDS in my head
like an endless echo

some say
(those without understanding)
that it is misplaced pride, egocentrism
but really
can one truly know anything else?

"they" do not exist
except through "i"

all creation
all existence
begins
and ends
with "i"

Jody Emond

live your lies
they are all you know
the truth would be too much
truth is hard
truth is cold
lies are as soft as you wish
as warm as you can make them

live the lies
maybe (although unlikely)
they may become truth
truth takes courage
truth takes strength

as long as you can convince yourself
the lies will do
but remember
eventually the lies will crumble
and only the truth
will remain
the alien, hard, cold truth
be prepared
be forewarned

YIN and yang
yes and no
black and white
male and female

honesty emerges
only when falsity is known

goodness emerges
only when evil is known

love
only when hate is known

such are the paradoxes
the contradictions
and the reality
of life

YESTERDAY a man came to me
he claimed to be a good man
because he had never seen evil
he claimed to be a strong man
because he had never known weakness
he claimed to be a wise man
because he had never known ignorance
he claimed to be a living man
because he had never known death

Jody Emond

i replied
you are a dead man
for all the same reasons

ENTER through me
my chest lies gaping
waiting for you to fill the void
i will be the instrument
upon which you shall play
so all ears present
shall hear the harmony
and equanimity of melody
the purity of notes

such that in turn
they shall whisper
this same melody as their own

in time
it shall be as common as breath
and as calm
as essential
and as natural
forever feeding the mind
with cool refreshing love
and acceptance

as they accept the air
so shall they accept one another
as they welcome it
so shall they welcome
a new peace

MY sanity is escaping like a greased pig
i hold tight
though there is little to grip
slowly i slip
into the nether regions
of my own mind and dreams

awake or asleep
the difference blurs
one coalescing into the other
the distinctions disappearing
into chaotic randomness
meaning has no meaning
illusion becomes reality
reality becomes illusion
together they form delusion

i drift further
from the continent of my birth
i become a lost jungle island
teeming with wildlife

Jody Emond

being all on the island
i kill myself
so i may live
losing myself in the contradiction

for now i build a bonfire
out of my own bones
praying its light is received
and we are rescued

HER mouth is closed
as is (more important)
her heart
it beats a singular beat
for no one to hear

alone she stands begging
to be understood
without explaining
a deep pain
that cannot be shared
or so she thinks

the simplistic beauty
that she possesses in abundance
is but a mask
to hide the true core
like the hard bark of a tree

she lives in fear
that no one would understand
the pain
she faces in her aloneness

awake child
and feel the pain
experience the beauty
live the living
wake up
and be

despite yourself
for in the end
you shall be victorious if you wish

THE WAY
what is it?
it is nothing

how do i achieve it?
by achieving nothing
how will i recognize it?
by seeing nothing

it is the voice that sings silence
the artist who paints an empty canvas

Jody Emond

it is the place
just before where you're going
just after where you've been

to see it
close your eyes
then ... close your eyes

to hear it
surround yourself with silence
then ... do not listen

to touch it
immerse yourself in nothing
then ... do not touch it

when you see the invisible
when you hear the inaudible
when you touch the untouchable
when you have scratched the unscratchable itch
when you have emptied your mind of
      everything
and opened it to everything
when your heart and mind
are one and the same
when you have accepted the serenity prayer
then you have made the first step

-

MUSIC blares
with certain uncertainty
echoing
the lost voices

here in the dark they stand alone
together
seeking nothing and finding everything
meaning exists in knowing first the
      meaningless
you stand alone
in the spotlight
not knowing
the surrounding darkness

and so pursue
a false reality
giving yourself
to closed eyes
and minds
accomplishing nothing

and so you go on

-

Jody Emond

HERE
they have found their world
for all who enter
are accepted
and so they must accept

though this reality
is shallow and fleeting
it is here
now

LOST are the parents who believe
as long as you have clothes on your back
it doesn't matter what they look like
if you have food in your belly
it doesn't matter what it is
if you don't get the shit kicked out of you
it doesn't matter how you are treated
as long as you are not despised
it doesn't matter whether you are loved

life needs to be more than this
being a parent needs to be more than this

BE formless
like water
without form, i have no definition
without definition, who am i?

definition is what limits
without it one can be anything

I SEEK the one teacher
i seek the true teacher
i seek the words of GOD himself

not the word transcribed or reiterated
or expounded by any source
other than GOD himself

i await the vision that comes
from the emptiness
of an unfulfilled desire to know
the one truth and meaning of all things

Jody Emond

GIVE me the freedom to be me
and i will give you the freedom to be you
the real YOU
the intrinsic you
the fundamental you

people are so much more interesting
when they give up the charade of society
from time to time
and allow themselves to be what they really feel

they are a GOD, a tree, a bug, a star
we are all more than we think
and less than what we are told to be
empty the mind, become the wind
going nowhere yet everywhere

feeling what
feeling how

you ask
i tell

reaching out
in blinded oblivion
begging in quiet obscurity

i seek the other half
of my infinite soul

i see and feel the same
uncompleted

LIFE of mediocrity
squelching the fires of my soul

words written for the deaf of ears and heart
echo without meaning through my mind

pulled in opposing directions
i seek to know the way to choose

in you
i find needed confidence
and control over life
my own

in you
i find rapture
and needed design

feeling your body
for lack of your heart
i find the warmth of human intimacy

Jody Emond

i have so craved

our bodies mesh as our souls may
should yours open

needing so
i let it be and wait

ultimate destiny
watch the dreams
shall they be?

ALONE we seek the light
of the hearth
to warm our weary bones
to show us a place to lay
in comfort and safety

so long we have walked
the dark misty streets
of this city we once called
home

once, long ago
we lost our way

so we pay
with the richest of our riches

pride
and spirit

losing track of the reality
we once embraced

shedding the illusion
a snake shedding its skin

painful and arduous

but at last
the freedom

IN this never-ending race
to keep up with the Joneses
we come that much closer
to becoming
the Mansons

Jody Emond

A BEER-induced satori
it will have to do

my eyes fill with tears
at the understanding
full and complete
beyond context
it is its own

i have seen the fulfillment
of all things
the perfection that is the process
and know i always did
in all ways

i see the world before me
for the mirage it is
and this serves the purpose
of calling the traveller farther
to the oasis
as does this reality
call us to go farther
to carry on
to the ultimate reality
to ourselves
for the world is both
the desert and the mirage

loneliness
darkness
coldness
one and the same

the glory of being the king
of a paradise island is lost
if the island is deserted

the richness of gold is lost
when no one can see its lustre

i remember the days past
when things were not so
when i walked with four feet
and when i slept
i laid two heads upon the pillow

I HAVE been much heavier than this
i have felt the weight of the world
crush my soul
and suck the breath from me

but now

i know
what is meant
by the "unbearable lightness of being"

the complete and utter sense
that all is as it could only be
and therefore
whatever the moment is
that is the perfect moment

for there is only one moment
and it exists
as all possibilities

everything that is possible
no matter how improbable
is possible
no matter how grand
or miniscule
no matter how simple
or complex

"REALITY is an illusion
albeit a very persistent one"
– Einstein

KNOW in these moments
of fear and dread
of worry and indecision
over the future to come

that what is lacking
is not strength or favour
but faith
and surrender to faith

TO be truth and compassion
without doctrine or dogma
to walk the path without a map
to spread the truth
without using the words of another
rather, to have the words bubble up
from the well of truth that is your soul
these are the challenges of the WAY

AT times
the loneliness i feel
is as the loneliness one experiences
when one's lover is absent
the feeling a part of you is missing

yet i have no part that is absent
i am whole

yet there is an ever-present void
formless and without origin

my arm is missing
i have two
i see them both
yet i know one is missing

if i look at my fingers
and slowly gaze up my arm
to my shoulder
i see that all is as it should be
yet i know i am missing an arm

as i have only two shoulders
i have no idea where i will put this arm
if and when i find it

all i know
is i am still missing an arm

THERE are no signs, no invitation
no certificate, no applause

there is only the choosing and then
the being

open yourself, decide
bravely

face to the sky
sun shining down
feel, embrace

take the step
and feel the freedom
in choosing

i have fixed the holes
the sieve is no more

now i become a cup
a chalice

to be filled drop by drop
with love and light

when the contents at last reach the brim
i shall hold the cup over your head
so you too may know the glory

Jody Emond

IN my secret life i am a king
and the world is my kingdom
i am a king with no need for a throne
i am a king only because i know the secrets of
      my life

in my secret life you are my wife
we live the country cottage and kids
we live tree tops and grasses swaying in the
      wind

in my secret life i am a sage
who fills your hearts and minds with truth and
      wisdom
so in time you may know the secrets of your life

in my secret life i am a star lost in the
      firmament
plummeting through infinity
lighting up the night sky
while caveman eyes peer skyward

in my secret life i am a god
i am ALL
and being so i choose to be ...

the ant that crawls up your arm

FROM my heart
to my will
from my will
to my hand
from my hand
to the paper
from the paper
to the fire
from the fire
to the ether
from the ether
to your heart
from your heart
to me
from me
to you
and then
to all the universe

don't you want to go nova?

ALL points in my past and future
flow through me
are me

boundless, indefinable
starting nowhere, going forever

Jody Emond

where does the chair end
and i begin?

the distinctions we make are practical
but are they the truth?

i am all and ALL is i

is it a wave or a particle?
... depends

none of it should, but it all does
the joke is on us
... we are the joke

images in an eye
reflections in a mind

a snake birthing itself
an Escher painting
art defining the artist defining the art

COME
let me dance with you

it's been so long
since i've been cheek to cheek

oh, i step on toes all the time
yet only metaphorically

but this time i promise
not to step on yours

come
do a tango
feel the life still in me

come
do a waltz
be my princess

come
dance a meringue
know my passion

come
dance with me
i won't step on your toes

I NEED to run
to flee
to hide

Jody Emond

from your ever-present voice
of condemnation

to find a place
of solitude
of solace

to find a place
of silence

to hear
the heavens
the truth

to hear
myself

AS waves ride the ocean
they become all things

for as wave hits wave
as water churns and contorts
in the swirling energies
of the world ocean

they become each other
waves become bubbles
of foam and froth

as they undulate they become
crests and troughs

as the wave moves
across the face of the mother/self/source
edges of white appear
and
dissolve

myriad forms
simplicity of substance

for in the ocean
all is ocean

I REMOVE my clothes
so my skin may be closer to your touch

i shed my skin
so my muscles may be closer to the object of
    their action

Jody Emond

i release my muscles
so i may lay my bones in a heap and fashion a
     bonfire

having given all that i am
i am finally free to be all that i am

TO smile easily
with softness

to speak with few words
on the lips

to know a thing as it is
not as you are

to focus on the aspect
still seeing the whole

to breathe lightly
with the entire body

markers on the WAY

I NEED the darkness
to find the LIGHT

i need the silence
to hear the VOICE

i need to be still
to feel the MOTION

i need to be hungry
to be filled with the TRUTH

i know it is the VOICE

because
though my skin is cold
i am warm

though i am in darkness
i see the LIGHT

though it is silent
i hear your call

and though i am weak
i stand to face the TRUTH

Jody Emond

NO mountains
no deserts
no majestic landscapes

i have not seen strange men
in distant lands
for they walk the same land as i

i have not travelled
stormy seas
for the treasures are washed
upon my shores

i have seen and lived
in my world,
the world of my birth

i have studied it as a wolf
studies his realm:
without word or wit
by sense and intuition

i have travelled through my time
i have experienced its wonders
i have tasted the fruit
where it lay

and i have let the flowing river
wash me

am i less a traveller
if the world travels over me?

I TURN
i face the sun

i fill my lungs
with the relaxed air of hope

i see the sun
and feel the warmth
in my soul

shedding frustrations
and fears
watching them fall
to the ground
like so many dead leaves

in the late days of autumn

Jody Emond

THE MYSTERY lies in all

for no matter how deep our knowledge
of a particular

there exists at all times a depth
to which we cannot descend

this knowledge is beyond
petty intellect and common sentiment

beyond words

it can only be known by
the MYSTERY that lies in each of us

I SEE you in your race
your haste

i wish to join
and share the pursuit

but the race you run
is of the three-legged kind

and though i have
two hearts and two stomachs

i have also
but two legs

HURRY up
get in line
take your place
watch the others
do as they
keep your place
hurry up
but not too much
step aside
go over there
stay here
stay there
stay where you are
stay
hurry up!

Jody Emond

TODAY
i release myself
from your yoke
your choke

today
i breath
the air fresh and new
not the canned air of rhetoric

THE ship is cast upon the churning waves
of the infinite sea
the captain calls the course
the navigator holds the rudder
wind fills the sails
the water seeks one direction
the wind seeks another
the ship wants only to hold together
the captain and crew
not to drown

for there are no mermaids to save lost sailors
and rocks surround the safety of the harbour

the captain calls:

the sea is a harsh mistress
but the only way between the worlds

lower the sails and let our mistress
guide our course

for our mistress is life itself
and we are always upon her waves

never adrift
for her currents guide us

WHO am i?
"i am" implies BEING

BEING implies static
unmoving, unchanging

i prefer BECOMING
changing, evolving, flowing

and so
when asked
"who are you?"

Jody Emond

i can only respond
"i am NOTHING
for i am always BECOMING"

AM i a fool
for seeing so much foolishness?

do i live in illusion
because i see so much delusion?

is it only the kind
who see kindness?
only the mad
who see madness?

is it the crying voice of weakness
or a roaring call to truth?

does anyone hear either?

there are a multitude of voices
should there not also be a multitude of ears
and hearts?

the kingdom you build around your heart
in your mind
cannot be shared

it would be better to have and share
a hovel

THERE is no truth
only many truths

there are no objects
only ideas

there is no path
only the WAY

there is no life
only being

there is no past, no future
only now

there is no me, no you
only us

there is nothing more
to say

Jody Emond

YOU know the truth
and with that
you build a lighthouse

from which to shine
the light of your truth
upon the world

the light you shine
is not without colour
and that colour is cast
upon all you survey

HOW can one hear
the soft words of truth
within the cacophony of illusion?

truth does not
scream or
stamp its feet
pull at you
demand attention

truth whispers

DON'T speak
    go back to yourself
and then
resign from yourself

fingers, mind, and heart
send them away

on errands of mercy

ALL the fruit
lies at your feet
    rotting
going back to the source

when the leaves have fallen
hack this tree to pieces
for though the fruit was unworthy
the wood is dry and brittle
good to burn

may it warm the empty bellies

Jody Emond

I RAGE

I RAGe

I RAge

I Rage

I rage

i rage

WHISPERS of truth
are heard through the cracks

all have cracks
all suffer

in this suffering
all are called to wisdom

YOU are not
what you think

you are not man
or woman
good or evil
wise or foolish

you are not what you suppose
you are not here
or there
now or then
whole or part

you are not
what you hope

you are not

INCREASINGLY you buy into
the market place
of comfort and distraction
paying in the only currency
of concern or matter
when you have found
so much comfort
you no longer see

your feet
when you have found
so much distraction
you no longer recall
your name
when finally you realize
you need to go home
you may not find
the house

WHO will be
the voice
of your
shadow?

I NEED
the darkness
as much
as the light
to see
the muted shadows
and to understand
the true
form

MEASURE your width
or measure your
height

notice
the depth
of your footprint
in the snow

hear only
the laughter
in the words
ignore
the message

IF you want to be wise
you have to look
at life through
bloody eyes
you have to take
the point of view
that sees the
hardest parts
the dirtiest parts
you have to suffer
through your vision

Jody Emond

I HAVE come
to the beach
not to build
castles of sand
but to watch
the tide
and what washes
upon the shore

i lay my back upon
the sand

fingers griping
waves at my feet

I HAVE
crawled
from the mud
to walk upon the land
and though
i have
become a bird
i shall
never
see the sky

WHEN the suicide fantasy ends
not with a good hospital scene
but with the click of the gun
it's time to worry

I'M not alive
i think so much
about living
i'm driving myself crazy

and what
kind of life
is that?

THERE can be
no solace
for the broken
of heart, mind, and soul

for there is no place
for it to reside

Jody Emond

FUNDAMENTALLY
i am a man who
finds life
dissatisfying

it's exhausting
to no end
this smile
made of skin

MY sanity
is slowly going
the way of
my hair
and shit
down the drain

with
colourful twists
and the soft gurgle
of drowning

THE biggest problem
with all the beer
i drink
is the damn
empty bottles

IT'S all just
so much
crap

how much
crap
do you take
in your soup?

I GOT a
double-barrelled shotgun
one barrel for beer
the other for a joint

now
i'm gonna get
loaded

Jody Emond

LONELINESS is
silent
a scream
from the depths
no dreamlike
shimmering light
above
only the blackness
below

i breath
the bubbles escaping
from my own
lungs

SHOULD a bird
blame the sky
because a cat
ate its flight feathers?

should a fish blame
the water
because a shark
ate one of its fins?

for that matter
should they blame
the cat
the shark
themselves
the fates?

or maybe
there is no blame

ENOUGH is enough

forty-two years ... to lead me to where
to here
to this place?

what a crock of shit
this is the loneliest place i have ever known
none of the roads have brought me where i
    hoped they would
not education, not love, not career
not obligation, not honor, not anything
i have come full circle to my beginnings

knowing nothing
unloved
going nowhere

Jody Emond

all it takes is a rope
a knife
a bullet

and enough pain to make the courage real
to make the courage do what it's time to do

i won't do it
i won't spend another year like this
for eighteen years my birthday has felt
as death
alone and empty
no witness

a bridge, a rock, a train
a pill, a cop, rat poison
a katana, a fucking steak knife

i understand nothing
and can tolerate even less
belonging nowhere
a part of nothing
uninvited, unwitnessed

crawling from the mud
i have done more alone
than most who started in the trees
and yet i am
insufficient, not enough, lacking

insane, demanding, hard, weak
too much, not enough

depleted, unnourished
broken, busted, twisted, crooked
my soul has become a used and discarded
    condom
that which could have become life
has instead become a black sticky stink
like my heart
like me

plant a tree in my corpse
maybe the fruit will be more useful
than the body was

NOBODY collects
broken vases

no bouquets
of flowers
missing petals

instead
let them
die

use the stench
of the
desiccated remains
to make
your life
smell
alive

CASTLES
built of
illusory bricks
held together with
wishful mortar

quick
we will build this
the house
of your ego

when it is done
we can find
shelter outside
in the shade
of the walls and towers
while you sleep on
feathers and down

we can drink the rain water
falling from your gutters
while you drink
our wine

CHARLIE Brown
meetings
melting my mind
wha wha wha wha wa wawawaw wha wha
wha wha wha wha wa wawawaw wha wha
rounded lips
making verbal
smoke rings

where's Lucy?
she could kick
the speaker
in the throat

THE metro doors
opened
there i was
in a GAP commercial
they were young

Jody Emond

eighteen at most
white, blond
and so
soap shiny

to the next train
can't get in
entrance blocked
dark shoes
dark jacket
dark hair
dark eyes
future power brokers
won't let me on
the train

YOU
with those
perfect breasts
speak to me
tell me
who you are
i want to know
i don't ask
that you
show them
to me

i ask only
that you speak
of what lies beneath.

I STAND here
with them
and i feel
nothing

humans
i am supposed
to be
one of them
and yet
i cannot talk
to any
of you

IN the morning
all was possible
but in the evening
when i saw the limits of the sun
i realized

Jody Emond

you were
the most perfect
for your beauty lasts
through the night.

THE fucked up
are those who
keep trying
to find
the real world

there is
no real world
there is only
perspective

and mine
is no more real
than yours

I AM a hammer
pounding
on the nail
at the tip of
your finger

i am the dog
barking mad
barking at you
to become
God

i am the
scream
that wakes you
in the middle
of your slumber
so you may see
the night

i am the poison
that you swallow down
all day, every day
filling you like a bladder
until you explode

i am the worms
that eat your rotting corpse
eyes, ears, and tongue
turn to dirt

THIS loneliness
kills me
as much

Jody Emond

as the pot
beer and
porn
i use to
kill it

HOW many words
does a poem
take?

a poem
can be only
one word
if it
gives you
the word

IT'S the weekend
i hate the fucking weekend
what the fuck good is it to me
no wife
no friends
no family
no motivation

no hobby
no calling
no joy
no relaxation
no fucking rope
no fucking bullets
no fucking gun
no fucking life
no fucking me

IN our secrets
we are all
monsters
for no one
hides their
greatness

IN the silence of
my mind
i hear only
the whispers
of a world
in pain
the strong suffer

in silence
and the weak
suffer in vain
for the ears
of the powerful
are deaf to the calls
of those in despair
and the voices
of need
are muffled
by greed

I AM a man
of dreams
and philosophy
not method
and technique

a man of style
and poetry
not class
and structure

a man of passion
and insanity
not control
and order

i am
a man
lost in
the machine

THE pictures
of you
like the memories
have been
dissolved
in a bath
of alcohol
and chemicals

it's a shame
my liver
and soul
had to go
the same way

IN this life
you only get
help
if you
suffer enough

did you do
everything
perfectly?

have you
sacrificed
all?

your power
your hope
your joy
your will
your life?

now
you will find
help

help
to die

THE only place
i want to go
is inward

countries
made of dreams

people
full of hope
and possibility

only as heavy
as i need to be
not to float away

tears and sweat
become
nourishing rain
and cleansing rivers

I KNOW what to do
with a dead body

but what do you do
with a dead soul?

nothing to bury
nothing to burn

nothing to feed
the vultures

Jody Emond

LONELINESS
is the meat grinder
of the soul

it reduces
you to shreds
and each shred
is examined
to find flaw

and each shred
is found
flawed

loneliness
is the meat grinder
of the soul

I HAVE been
the sun
above
shedding light
and warmth

i have been
the dirt
beneath
giving traction
and support

but
the hardest to be
is the one
who walks
beside you
in the light
and on the dirt

I USED to travel
the highways
in your eyes
to the softest parts
of my soul

now i am lost
and all the roads
lead to
the same
cliff

Jody Emond

LET it rain
if love was rain
i would strip and
run naked outside

if love was snow
i would throw myself
into it and make angels

if love was air
i would fill my lungs
and float to the roof of the world

but love
is you
and you are not here

and so
neither
am i

standing
on the outside
always
looking in

i've grown tired
kneecapped and blinded
i can finally rest

ABOUT THE AUTHOR

Jody Emond has a degree in psychology. He is a fan of science and philosophy, and his book-shelves are filled with science fiction, graphic novels, and comic books. He is a single dad and a computer/LAN support specialist with the Canadian government, sentenced to thirty-five years of Kafkaesque decision making by "superiors" before full pension. *Flotsam and Jetsam* is his first book of poetry. He lives in Montreal.